Elena Grigorieva

The Indispensable Eight

The Birth and Rise of Kingdom Animalia

novum ◢ pro

This book is also
available as
e-book.

www.novum-publishing.co.uk

© 2022 novum publishing

ISBN 978-3-99131-569-8
Editing: Hugo Chandler, BA
Cover photos: Wavebreakmedia Ltd,
Ivan Kruk | Dreamstime.com,
Elena Grigorieva
Cover design, layout & typesetting:
novum publishing
Internal illustrations: Elena Grigorieva

www.novum-publishing.co.uk

Climate neutral
Print product
ClimatePartner.com/16547-2201-1002

Contents

From Unicellular Protozoans to Multicellular Metazoans

Around 600 million years ago our planet Earth was very different from what it is now. There were no animals. Instead, there were various tiny, unicellular creatures which lived in the warm waters of the ancient oceans and lakes. Some of them had a long, tail-like structure – a flagellum, which they used for swimming. Biologists call these creatures protozoans.

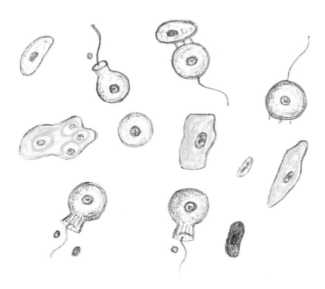

In order to get nutrients essential for living, the protozoans ate other cells and organic structures. While feeding on bigger cells or food particles, the protozoans gathered into groups, or colonies. Eventually, some cells within such groups divided but remained connected to each other. This led to the formation of stable aggregates, where cells multiplied and grew as a single organism. Such multicellular organisms are called metazoans, and it is believed that the very first metazoans were the ancestors of all animals on Earth. They gave rise to the kingdom Animalia and marked the beginning of animal evolution.

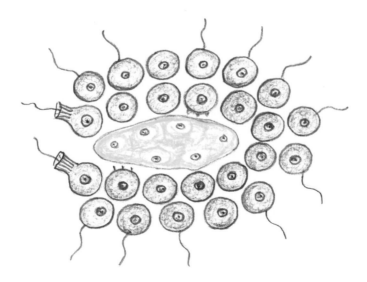

How Cells Specialise

In the course of evolution, cells in some metazoans began to vary from each other in structure and function. This process is called cell specialisation and can be briefly described as follows.

Cells located on the outer side of metazoan organisms became more tightly connected to each other and were more resistant to the harmful effects of the environment, thereby protecting the inner-located cells. Over time, the outer cells gave rise to the epidermal cells, which form the outermost protective layer of the skin in complex animals.

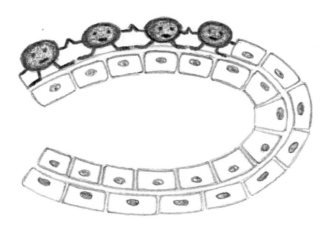

Some cells became specifically sensitive to the environmental signals such as chemical substances, light, sound, or pressure. Moreover, they became able to transmit the signals to other cells of the organism, thereby giving rise to the first sensory and motor neurons.

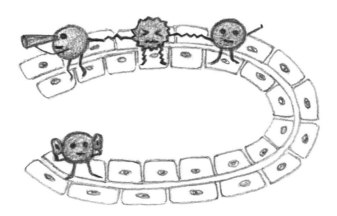

Some cells became able to contract and relax in response to the signals from the neurons and, with the help of support cells, that allowed the metazoan to perform essential movements and keep a certain shape. Such kinds of cells gave rise to the first muscle and support cells.

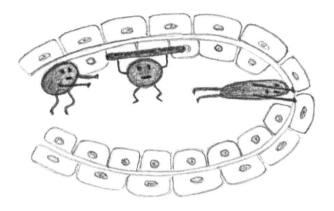

Cells lining the inside cavity of the metazoan, and being in direct contact with food, specialised in digestion of organic particles by changing them into simple forms that could be easily used by all cells of the organism. These cells became the first digestive cells of the gut.

Metazoan cells need oxygen for energy production by a process of respiration, so some cells specialised in obtaining oxygen from the environment in larger quantities and in gas exchange, in order to fulfil the needs of the whole organism. These cells gave rise to the respiratory cells of the gills and lungs.

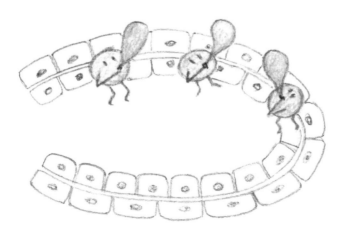

Some cells specialised in delivering oxygen and nutrients to every other cell of the organism, and also protected against harmful viruses, bacteria and other intruders. These cells became the first circulatory and immune cells.

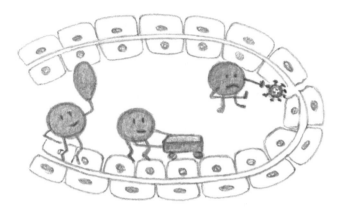

Some cells specialised in sorting out the products of cellular metabolism and excreting unneeded molecules out of the organism. These cells gave rise to the excretory cells of the kidneys.

And finally, two kinds of haploid cells (containing only one set of chromosomes) – eggs and
sperm cells – became responsible for giving
birth to a new metazoan organism by means
of sexual reproduction. These cells gave rise
to the first reproductive cells.

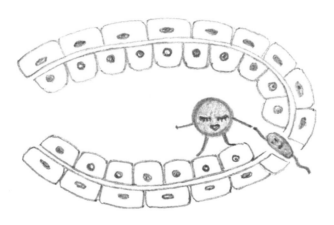

How Animals Evolve

The division of cells to serve a specific function has played a key role in the evolution of metazoans and in the appearance of different animal species. Especially important has been the way by which metazoans reproduce, in particular, sexual reproduction. The genetic material of the nuclear DNA, which is carried into the egg cell by the sperm cell from the male organism, as well as molecular changes (or mutations) in the genomes of these cells, enable fast transmission of novel features and traits to new-born organisms. Sexual reproduction has led to an enormous varieties of animal species, which are characterised by different body structures, behaviours and habitats. After around 70 million years since the appearance of the first metazoans, Earth has become inhabited by animals as primitive as sponges and as complex as vertebrates.

It should be noted that the evolution of animals is a continuous process, which is influenced by many environmental conditions. Over the course of time, due to extreme changes in climate and other unfavourable factors, many animal species became extinct, while many others arose later, and many new species will appear in the future.

Biologists have described and classified over three million living animal species and 35 major body plans (or phyla), based on animals' body structure and ways of development. Although profoundly different from each other, all animals share a common ancestor, the protozoan, and the eight types of cell specialisation have remained as the metazoan-specific features of the vast majority of animal species.

The Major Categories of Metazoan Cells

With the exception of sponges and some other primitive metazoans which lack specialised tissues, and in which the processes of breathing, delivery of nutrients, and excretion are carried out in them by the diffusion of molecules, more complex animals are formed by cells which can be distributed into eight major groups, or categories. Each category includes cells which are characterised by specific visible features, as well as physical and biochemical properties that are acquired during animals' development through the process of cell differentiation. These categories are: (1) epidermal cells; (2) nerve cells; (3) muscle and support cells; (4) digestive cells; (5) respiratory cells; (6) circulatory and immune cells; (7) excretory cells; and (8) reproductive cells. The simplified pictures of cells representing the major categories in complex animals are as follows.

The epidermal cells

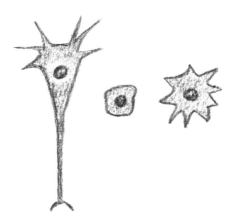

The nerve cells

The muscle and support cells

The digestive cells

The respiratory cells

The circulatory and immune cells

The excretory cells

The reproductive cells

In the course of animal evolution there has been a significant increase in the diversity of cell types within the major categories, that led to a gradual growth of structural and functional complexity of animal organisms. Thus, animals such as mammals account for more than 200 different types of cells, which form various tissues, complex organs and body systems. It should be noted that sizes of cell bodies have remained approximately the same, and that animals, whether they be a small mouse or a giant whale, differ in the number of cells they are made up of rather than the cell's size.

The different types of cells within the major categories in a mammalian organism can be described as follows.

The epidermal cells form the epidermis, the outermost layer of cells covering the whole body. These cells are arranged in several layers and serve to protect the organism from environmental effects. The epidermal cells produce a protein called keratin, which gradually accumulates in the cells and contributes to their barrier function. The upper keratinised cells die eventually and are replaced by the new proliferating and differentiating cells located at the base of the epidermis. The epidermal cells also form the accessory structures such as hairs, nails and skin glands.

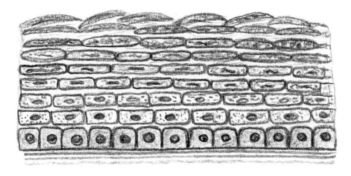

The epidermal cells of the skin

The nerve cells are a group of cells which include the sensory and motor neurons, interneurons, glial cells, and receptor cells. These cells differ in their function and structure. Neurons are characterised by special projections from the cell body – dendrites and an axon – through which they communicate with other cells by receiving and sending signalling molecules called neurotransmitters. Neurons can generate electrical signals, which are transmitted along the axons. Glial cells play special roles to support and protect the neurons. Receptor cells specifically detect external and internal stimuli and transmit the signals to sensory neurons. There are also neuroendocrine cells which secrete hormones. The different types of nerve cells form the brain, spinal cord, numerous nerves, ganglia, and sensory structures.

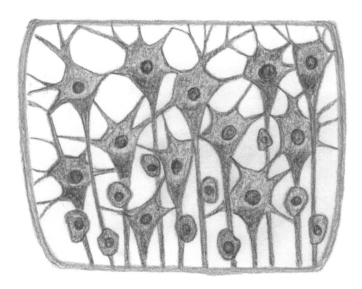

The nerve cells of the ganglion

The muscle and support cells are responsible for the body's strength and movements. Muscle cells contain special contractile structures which allow them to change their shape in response to neuronal signals. Muscle cells can be smooth or striated and are usually attached to different types of support cells. Support cells form various connective tissues, such as bone, cartilage, tendons, and fibrous connective tissues. Support cells secrete special proteins such as collagen and elastin and other substances which form the extracellular matrix and are responsible for the physical properties of the tissues. Support cells such as fat cells (also called brown and white adipocytes) accumulate and store fat as a source of energy.

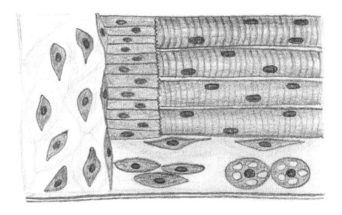

The muscle and connective tissues

The digestive cells specialise mainly in secreting various enzymes and other active substances that convert food into simple molecules which can be used by all cells of the organism. The digestive cells constitute different parts of the gut (oesophagus, stomach, small and large intestine) and accessory organs such as salivary glands, the liver and the pancreas. They differ in their structure, secretions and functions. For example, the digestive cells of the small and large intestine absorb nutrients and transfer them into the blood. Undigested food is disposed out of the gut.

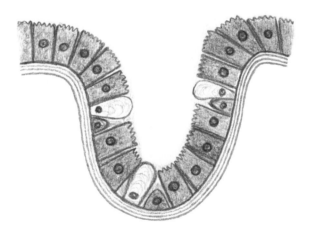

The digestive cells of the gut

The respiratory cells form the lungs, the main functional units of which are the alveolar sacs filled with air containing oxygen. These cells provide the gaseous exchange between the environment and the red blood cells. Some of the respiratory cells secrete special substances called surfactants, which keep the alveoli open, and some of the cells have cilia, whose role is to moisten and clear up the airways.

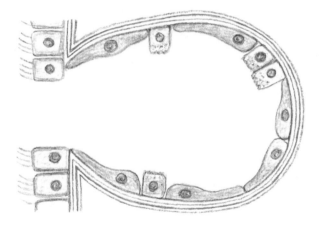

The respiratory cells of the lung

The circulatory and immune cells include the endothelial cells, which form the innermost layer of the vessels and heart chambers, the red and white blood cells, the immune cells of the lymphoid organs, and the cells of the bone marrow. The red blood cells, or erythrocytes, contain the protein haemoglobin which allows the transport of oxygen and carbon dioxide. The different types of white blood cells and immune cells play special protective roles against harmful microorganisms, eliminate dead cells, and provide the immune response.

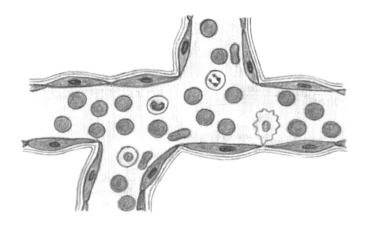

The blood cells within the vessel

The excretory cells form the kidneys, the main functional units of which are the nephrons, where the blood is filtered and the urine is formed. The excretory cells specifically select various solute molecules and play an important role in water and salt balance. The urine containing unneeded molecules passes through special ducts into the bladder, where it is concentrated and then removed out of the organism.

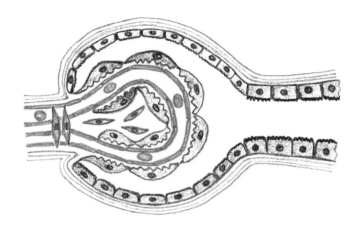

The excretory cells of the kidney

The reproductive cells constitute the female and male sex organs, where the egg and sperm cells develop. These cells differ from each other. The egg cell is relatively large and has all the cellular elements. The sperm cell is very small, consisting of a head with nuclear chromosomes and a tail – the flagellum, which allows this cell to move fast. The egg cells (also called oocytes) develop in female ovaries consisting of numerous follicles. Each follicle contains only one oocyte, which is nurtured by the follicular cells. The sperm cells develop in male testes.

The mature egg and sperm cells are released from their sites of development to be joined together. When the egg cell and the sperm cell are fused, the newly formed fertilised egg starts to proliferate within the female's uterus and develops into a new mammalian organism through the process of embryogenesis.

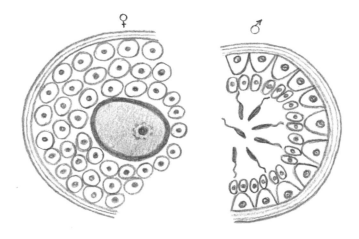

*The reproductive cells
of the ovary and testis*

How Animals Develop

The process of embryogenesis of a complex organism such as a mammalian includes simultaneous development of two parts: the embryo proper and the extraembryonic structures. The embryo proper undergoes different stages of its organisation, which resemble the evolutionary changes in the complexity of animal structure. Initially, the early embryonic cells become arranged into two layers: the ectoderm and the endoderm. A third layer, the mesoderm, is then formed between these two layers. The embryonic cells intensively divide, differentiate, and form different types of tissue.

In general, the tissues are classified as epithelial tissues, connective tissues, muscle tissues, and nervous (or neural) tissues. In epithelial tissues (or epithelium) cells tightly connect to each other, polarise, and build up barriers which separate the different body parts from the external and internal environment, and at the same time provide necessary communications.

Epithelial tissues are formed, for example, by the epidermal cells, digestive cells, and excretory cells. Cells of the connective tissues become separated from each other by the extracellular matrix; they provide mechanical strength and protection to other tissues in the body. Connective tissues are formed by the support cells. Muscle tissues are formed by contractile muscle cells. Neural tissues are formed by the nerve cells.

The different types of cells and tissues form the external and internal organs. During the formation of each organ, the embryonic cells communicate with each other by secreting specific signalling molecules which can either attract or repel certain cells. For example, mesoderm-derived muscle cells release the molecules that attract ectoderm-derived nerve cells. The latter extend towards the muscle cells and form the neuro-muscular junctions, through which they control the muscle's actions. Similarly, the endothelial cells are attracted by the molecules from the muscle cells and form adjacent vessels which supply the muscle with the blood. So, the muscle as an organ consists of different types of cells from three different categories. All organs (the heart, stomach, liver, kidneys,

and others) are formed by such a principle –
through cell-type-specific signalling molecules
which unite different types of cells and tissues,
thereby generating the architecture, or mor-
phology, of the developing organs.

The Body Systems

At the end of embryogenesis, the different types of cells, tissues and organs are combined to form the body systems. There are eight major body systems, which, in general, play the same indispensable roles as the major categories of metazoan cells. The body systems of a mammalian organism are as follows.

The skin, or integumentary system. This system consists of two layers of tissue. The outmost layer, the epidermis, is formed by the epidermal cells and accessory structures, such as hairs, nails and skin glands. The second layer, the dermis, is formed by the nerve cells, the muscle and support cells, and the circulatory and immune cells.

The nervous system comprises the brain, spinal cord, neuronal ganglia, nerves, and sensory structures such as olfactory epithelium in the nose, the retina in the eyes, and the inner ears. All these morphological structures also include the circulatory and immune cells, and the muscle and support cells.

The musculoskeletal and support system consists of various muscles, bones, cartilages, tendons, ligaments, fibrous connective tissue, and adipose tissue. The organs and morphological structures of this system also comprise the circulatory and immune cells, and the nerve cells.

The digestive system includes the mouth, salivary glands, oesophagus, stomach, pancreas, liver, and the intestines. The organs of this system are formed by the digestive cells, the circulatory and immune cells, the muscle and support cells, and the nerve cells.

The respiratory system includes the trachea and lungs. These organs are formed by the respiratory cells, and also comprise the circulatory and immune cells, the muscle and support cells, and the nerve cells.

The circulatory and immune system includes the heart, vessels, blood, and lymphoid organs such as the spleen, thymus and lymph nodes.

The organs and morphological structures of this system combine the circulatory and immune cells, the muscle and support cells, and the nerve cells. The system is subdivided into the cardiovascular system and the immune system.

The excretory system includes the kidneys, ureters, the urinary bladder, and the urethra. This system comprises the excretory cells, the circulatory and immune cells, the muscle and support cells, and the nerve cells.

The reproductive system includes the ovaries, producing the egg cells in females, and the testes, producing the sperm cells in males. The accessory reproductive, or genital, organs comprise the epidermal cells, the muscle and support cells, the circulatory and immune cells, and the nerve cells.

Throughout the lifetime of a mammalian organism, the body systems constantly interact with each other by means of biologically active molecules, such as hormones, which are produced by endocrine cells which are found in all these systems. Such communications between the body systems are very important. Therefore, the cells and organs that secrete hormones have been classified as the **endocrine system**. The interactions between the body systems define the internal stability, or homeostasis, of the whole organism.

Animal Anatomy

The following pictures represent the anatomy of animals belonging to evolutionary distant groups. These are the squid, the fish, the frog, the bird, and the cat. The different body systems of these animals are marked by the same colour used in the drawings showing the eight major categories of metazoan cells. So, the integumentary system is brown, the nervous system – pink, the musculoskeletal and support system – mahogany (this system is shown by the line only), the digestive system – green, the respiratory system – blue, the circulatory and immune system – red, the excretory system – violet, and the reproductive system – orange. The pictures show that animals from molluscs to mammals comprise the eight indispensable categories of metazoan cells and body systems.

Squid
Squid comprise a group of invertebrate animals that belong to the phylum Mollusca, the second-largest phylum after the Arthropoda. There are over 300 different species of squid, which live in marine waters. They vary significantly in

their size and can grow from ten centimetres to ten metres. The squid's elongated body comprises simple but distinct internal organs protected by the mantle. The head has two large eyes and a mouth surrounded by several short arms and two longer tentacles. The respiratory cells form the gills; the organ that allows squid to breathe in water.

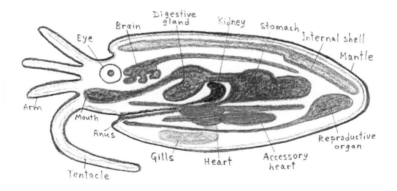

Squid anatomy

Fish
Fish comprise a group of vertebrate animals that belong to the phylum Chordata. There are around 34,000 species, which live in fresh and in marine waters. Fish are more complex than squid. They comprise organs and anatomical structures that contain all the major

body systems, although evolutionary fish are less complex than the four classes of air-breathing vertebrate animals – amphibians, reptiles, birds, and mammals. Fish are characterised by the body features that allow these animals to live in water. Thus, the epidermal cells of fish skin form scales covering the whole body. The fins, as part of the musculoskeletal system, help fish to move in water and the respiratory cells of the gills utilise oxygen dissolved in water.

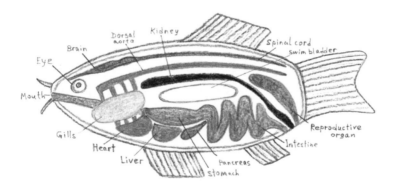

Fish anatomy

Frogs
Frogs compose a large and diverse group of amphibians. They are widely distributed on Earth and live in water and on land. Frogs

have smooth, moist skin, large protruding eyes, strong hind feet, and no tail. Frogs have organs and anatomical structures which are found in the major body systems characteristic of vertebrate animals.

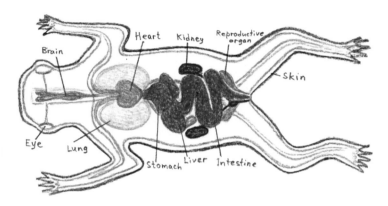

Frog anatomy

Birds
Birds are a group of vertebrate animals called Aves. There are about 10,400 living species of birds. These warm-blooded animals are related more to reptiles than to mammals. Their bodies include well-defined organs and anatomical structures of the eight major body systems. The characteristic features of birds are the feathers on the skin and the wings – the modified forelimbs which allow birds to fly.

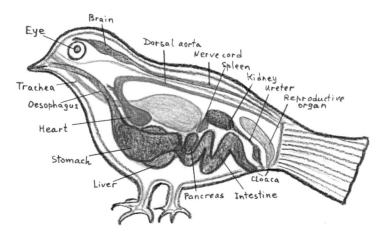

Bird anatomy

Mammals

Mammals are evolutionary-wise the most advanced vertebrate animals with complex body systems. There are over 6,400 living species of mammals, including human beings. The characteristic features of mammals are hairs or fur of the skin, the highly-developed nervous system, and the mammary glands. Mammals are adapted to live in almost every corner of the planet. Mammalian species vary significantly in size, ranging from four centimetres (some species of shrews and mice) to thirty metres (the Blue whale).

Cats form a group of small carnivorous mammals, which were domesticated as pets several thousand years ago. These animals are characterised by their social nature and relatively high intelligence.

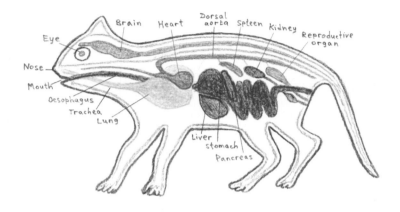

Cat anatomy

The rise of the animal kingdom resulted in the appearance of the first human beings around 2.5 million years ago. Humans of the species *Homo sapiens* stand out from all other mammals. The main characteristics of humans are cognition and creative behaviour. These important qualities have developed not only as a result of the evolutionary process but also by means of natural selection; a result of a series of evolutionary events which have led to new ways and styles of human life. Humans have become able to learn, memorise and record almost everything that surrounds them. Humans can create and change almost everything they desire. Over a relatively short period of evolutionary time, humans have become masters of the whole world.

There is rising curiosity about the future of human beings, and the simple answer is that the future of humankind is in the hands of humans. The possibilities are infinite.

The author

Elena Grigorieva was born in 1954 in Kuibyshev Russia. She attended Moscow State University and attained a PhD in histology, anatomy and embryology. She was employed as a scientific officer at the MRC National Institute for Medical Research in London. She was involved in the histological analysis of various genetically modified animal models. After her retirement in 2011, she continues to participate in scientific research. She has incorporated this knowledge into her writing.

Her favourite activities are reading, watching documentary films about the universe and biodiversity on Planet Earth; travelling to various countries, experiencing and learning about different cultures, going to museums and theatres. Her special skills are sewing, knitting and drawing. Since her schooldays she was interested in the structure of human and animal bodies and the evolutionary aspects of life.

She is married and has two daughters. This is her first book.

The publisher

*He who stops
getting better
stops being good.*

This is the motto of novum publishing, and our focus
is on finding new manuscripts, publishing them and
offering long-term support to the authors.
Our publishing house was founded in 1997, and since
then it has become THE expert for new authors and
has won numerous awards.

**Our editorial team will peruse each manuscript
within a few weeks free of charge and without
obligation.**

You will find more information about
novum publishing and our books on the internet:

w w w . n o v u m - p u b l i s h i n g . c o . u k